Native American Peoples

CREE

Mary Stout

Gareth Stevens Publishing
A WORLD ALMANAC EDUCATION GROUP COMPANY

Please visit our web site at: www.garethstevens.com
For a free color catalog describing Gareth Stevens Publishing's list of high-quality books
and multimedia programs, call 1-800-542-2595 (USA) or 1-800-387-3178 (Canada).
Gareth Stevens Publishing's fax: (414) 332-3567.

Library of Congress Cataloging-in-Publication Data

Stout, Mary, 1954-
    Cree / by Mary Stout.
      p. cm. — (Native American peoples)
    Summary: Describes the origin, history, language, daily life, and future prospects
of the Cree Indians of Canada.
    Includes bibliographical references and index.
    ISBN 0-8368-3703-7 (lib. bdg.)
    1. Cree Indians—Juvenile literature. [1. Cree Indians. 2. Indians of North
America—Canada.] I. Title. II. Series.
E99.C88S87   2003
971.2004'973—dc21   2003045708

First published in 2004 by
Gareth Stevens Publishing
A World Almanac Education Group Company
330 West Olive Street, Suite 100
Milwaukee, WI 53212 USA

Copyright © 2004 by Gareth Stevens Publishing.

Produced by Discovery Books
Project editor: Valerie J. Weber
Designer and page production: Sabine Beaupré
Photo researcher: Rachel Tisdale
Native American consultant: D. L. Birchfield, J. D., Associate Professor of Native American
  Studies at the University of Lethbridge, Alberta
Maps and diagrams: Stefan Chabluk
Gareth Stevens editorial direction: Mark Sachner
Gareth Stevens art direction: Tammy Gruenewald
Gareth Stevens production: Beth Meinholz and Jessica L. Yanke

Photo credits: Corbis: cover, pp. 9 (bottom), 13 (top), 14, 18 (top), 19, 21 (top), 23, 24, 25
(both), 26 (both), 27; Courtesy of the Library of Congress: p. 5; North Wind Picture Archives:
pp. 6, 8; Peter Newark's American Pictures: pp. 7, 9 (top), 10 (both), 11, 12, 13 (bottom), 20
(top); Native Stock: pp. 16, 17, 18 (bottom), 20 (bottom), 21 (bottom).

Printed in the United States of America

1 2 3 4 5 6 7 8 9 07 06 05 04 03

Cover: A colorfully dressed and painted Cree child waves a Canadian flag during a visit from
Prince Charles of Great Britain.

Contents

Words that appear in the glossary are printed in **boldface** type the first time they appear in the text.

Origins

Land of the Crees

The Cree **Nation** is made up of numerous small hunter-gatherer bands who once roamed a huge area in Canada east of the Hudson and James Bays, as far west as Alberta and as far south as Lake Superior. Today the largest Native American nation in Canada (where Indian tribes are called First Nations), over 200,000 Crees live in Canada alone, and many others live in the United States.

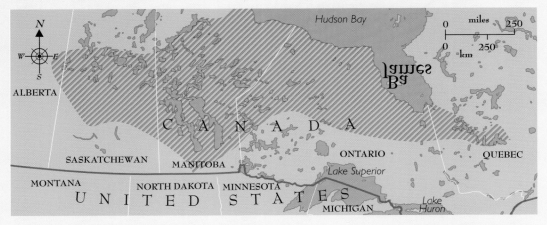

As the orange areas show, before 1500 Cree territory stretched from what is today western Alberta to eastern Quebec in Canada. Some Cree bands gradually moved onto the Great Plains in what is now the northern United States.

A Traditional Origin Story

Like many ancient peoples, for generations traditional Crees have told a story about how they came to their lands. In the beginning, the Crees lived in the land above. A man and a woman decided to go to the land below. As a spider lowered them on a line, it warned them not to look down until they reached the ground. Of course, they looked, so the line stopped, leaving them stuck atop a tall tree. They asked a passing caribou, lynx, bear, and wolverine all to carry them down, but only the bear and wolverine would help. The couple followed the bear, which taught them everything about how to stay alive. According to this origin story, all the Crees are descended from these two.

No one knows how and when Indians came to North America. Some scientists believe they are descended from people who crossed the Bering Strait along a landmass that may have stretched between Asia and North America during the last Ice Age. Others suggest that Indians sailed across the seas, landed in South America, and walked up to North America. However they got to the continent, scientific evidence proves that the Crees lived in their traditional lands since at least about A.D. 900.

This Woodlands Cree man is using a horn made of birch bark to imitate a moose call.

The Ojibwe and French fur traders called them *Kristineaux,* later shortened to "Cree." The Crees called themselves "Nehiyawak," meaning "exact people."

The Cree tribe was divided into two major cultures. The culture of the Western Woods Crees, also called the Woodland Crees, was based upon hunting and trapping in the forests of the cold north. Buffalo hunting formed the basis of the Plains Crees' culture.

The Cree Language

Cree is a Central Algonquian language with many different **dialects**.

Cree	Pronunciation	English
atim	uh-tim	dog
ta'n(i)si	tah-nih-sih	hello
tahka'ya'w	tuhk-ah-yow	(it's) cold
mispon	mis-pohn	snow
wa'skahikan	wah-skuh-hi-kun	house

Chapter 2

History

Western Woods Cree History

The Western Woods Crees included many different Cree bands. For hundreds of years, they lived off the land by hunting and trapping animals. Those living around the bays and lakes depended more upon fishing for food. All these bands spoke a similar language.

During the 1800s, fur dealers arrived by wagon and boat at the Hudson's Bay trading post to buy and sell furs bound for Europe.

The huge demand for furs in Europe brought the first French traders to Cree country, where they set up trading posts. Excellent hunters and trappers, the Crees exchanged beaver pelts for trade goods, such as guns, knives, pots, pans, and other household items, first with the French and then with the British.

Trading posts also hired many Crees as hunters to supply them with meat. For a short time, the Crees were a rich, powerful tribe. As the supply of animals dwindled, however, the Crees had to keep moving south and west looking for more game.

They were so busy hunting and trapping for the traders that many were no longer completely self-sufficient and became unable to live entirely off the land. By 1717, many

Western Woods Crees depended upon the Hudson's Bay Company for guns, cloth, blankets, and for some of their food, changing their traditional lifestyle.

When Europeans arrived in North America, they brought diseases that killed more Native Americans than all other causes combined, including war. In 1781, a **smallpox epidemic** wiped out about half of the Cree population.

Hudson's Bay Company

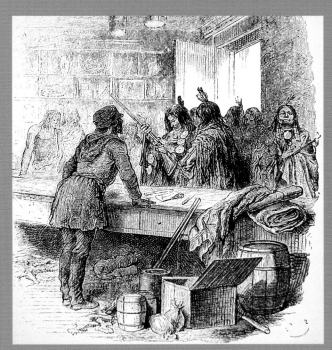

In this drawing from 1845, the Crees trade their furs for guns at the Hudson's Bay Company trading post.

In 1670, the British started the Hudson's Bay Company (HBC) in northern Canada to trade in furs for coats, hats, muffs, and capes. In 1821, HBC merged with its rival, the North West Company, and became the world's largest fur-trading business, expanding its territory throughout Canada. HBC governed a huge area and the Natives living there until 1870, when it turned over all of its lands to Canada.

HBC changed the lives of the Canadian Natives, hiring them to trap and hunt and exchanging many European goods for furs and skins. Once beaver hats lost popularity in Europe in the mid-nineteenth century, the demand for furs declined. HBC became a successful Canadian department store, but Native fur trappers lost both their jobs and the means to pay for the European goods they depended upon.

Jesuit missionaries coming to preach to the fur traders and Native Americans. Many had little respect for the traditional Native spiritual practices they were trying to replace.

Changes for the Western Woods Crees

Native communities sprang up around trading posts, with religious **missions** located nearby; these areas became social centers and semipermanent homes for the formerly wandering Crees. The missionaries tried to **convert** the Western Woods Crees to Christianity. Giving up their traditional religion and lifestyle, many Crees also abandoned their traditional handmade goods for Canadian cloth, pots, pans, and other items.

Throughout the nineteenth century, however, few Europeans settled in the cold north, and the Indians continued to use their traditional hunting grounds. Then lumber companies disturbed the heavily forested lands. In **treaties** signed between 1876 and 1906, the Western Woods Crees traded most of their traditional lands to the Canadian government in exchange for **reserves** and promised **social services**.

From 1920 to 1940, many diseases new to the Crees, such as measles and flu, hit them hard. After World War II (1939–1945), government services such as schools and health

The Crees are more sprightly, always in motion, always dancing or singing. Both [Crees and Assiniboines] are brave and love war.

From a letter written in 1706 by Father Pierre-Gabriel Marest comparing the Assiniboine and Cree people

clinics grew up around the old trading posts, forming villages. The Crees lived in these villages year-round, though the men left on hunting trips during the winter.

By the 1940s, the Crees depended upon the Canadian government for their living. The market for fur was gone, and fewer Western Woods Crees lived in traditional ways. Beginning in the late 1940s until the 1970s, most Cree children were sent away to boarding schools where they learned English. Since they didn't live with their families, however, they forgot how to speak Cree and learned no traditional skills.

Northern Crees traditionally came to the Great Whale River during the summer to hunt beluga whales, trade, and visit. These people were photographed in 1970.

Women's Work: Making Buckskin

The Western Woods Cree men depended upon Cree women to turn animal hides into leather for clothing. Women rubbed the animal hide with a mixture of animal brains, fat, and liver and then soaked it in water. They softened the stiff hide by rubbing it over a rough stone, then stretched and pulled it. When the hide was soft, they could sew it into clothing — shirts, pants, and dresses. Once the Crees became dependent on woven cotton cloth, such traditional skills began to disappear.

A woman cleans a caribou hide at a Cree bush camp.

An 1826 painting by Peter Rindisbacher shows a Plains Cree man on foot chasing a buffalo with his dogs. Crees often hunted buffaloes by frightening the animals so that they ran into pens or into a marsh, trapping them and making them easy targets.

Plains Cree History

As the Crees expanded to their territory's southwest between 1670 and 1810, the Plains Crees emerged as a distinct group. The scarcity of winter game had forced them to move onto the Plains in southern Saskatchewan and Alberta to hunt buffalo. They also became agents for the European traders, exchanging goods for furs with other tribes to bring into the trading posts.

Allied with the Blackfeet Indians, the Crees began to live like other Plains Natives.

Plains Cree families lived in tepees fashioned from twelve to twenty buffalo hides sewn together with sinew and supported by poles.

Buffalo skins provided clothing and shelter, while buffalo meat fed the people. In the northern woods, the canoe had been the most important form of transportation, but for hunting on the plains, horses were necessary.

Between 1810 and 1850, the Plains Crees moved farther into the Plains areas but had problems getting enough horses — both for transportation and, in their new lifestyle, for status. This time, known as the "Horse Wars," saw the Crees stealing or fighting to capture horses from other tribes.

Mustatem Moutiapec (Horse Roots) was a Plains Cree Indian photographed at the turn of the century, after the buffalo began to disappear.

Wars and Treaties

Between 1850 and 1880, buffaloes began to vanish from the Plains, killed by Americans for their hides. Because the animals disappeared first from Canada, the Crees entered other tribes' territories in the United States to hunt buffalo, which led to warfare. The Blackfeet drove the Crees out of their territory in today's southern Canada and northern Montana, defeating their former allies at the Battle of Old Man River in 1871.

Returning to Canada without buffalo, the starving Plains Crees requested a treaty with the Canadian government. In exchange for Cree lands, the treaty promised them farming tools, seeds, a yearly payment, and schools. Unfortunately, the government provided poor-quality grain and tools so farming was difficult.

It may truly be said that they exist on the buffalo, and their knowledge of the habits of this animal is consequently essential to their preservation. . . . Next to the buffalo the horse is the mainstay of the prairie Indians. . . . Next to the horse, the dog is the Prairie Indians' most valuable friend.

Professor Henry Youle Hind during his 1858 exploration, published in Narrative of the Canadian Red River

Allying with the Métis

In 1885, Louis Riel led the Métis (who were the **descendants** of Native Americans and Europeans, usually French) in an uprising against the Canadian government because it refused to admit that the Métis had any claims to the lands they had lived on all their lives. Plains Cree chiefs Poundmaker and Big Bear sympathized with the Métis. Some members of Big Bear's band killed nine priests and settlers at Frog Lake on the Alberta–Saskatchewan border. Eight Cree warriors were convicted of murder. Both Big Bear and Poundmaker were convicted of **treason** for planning to overthrow the Canadian government and sentenced to three years in prison. Big Bear's son led the rest of his band across the border to Montana, where they joined an Ojibwe (also known as Chippewa or Anishinaabe) band; their descendants continue to live there today.

Louis Riel spent his life fighting for the rights of the Métis.

This painting by Paul Kane shows Blackfeet chief Big Snake being killed by an unnamed Cree war chief. The Canadian artist created this work from his imagination; Big Snake actually died after the painting was completed.

By the late 1800s, Christian missionaries had become an important influence on the Plains Crees; they converted many to Christianity and worked to end traditional religious practices. From 1884 to 1921, for example, the Sun Dance was outlawed in Canada, and many other traditional ceremonies had to be held in secret. World War II (1939–1945) saw more and better social services for the Plains Crees, and returning war veterans became new leaders within the Cree community. Plains Cree children went to missionary schools, while their parents, no longer able to live off the land, looked to paying jobs and government allowances to help them survive.

Poundmaker

Called Pitikwahanapiwiyin by the Crees, Poundmaker was adopted by a Blackfeet chief.

Poundmaker was born in 1842 and was named for his ability to make pens to trap buffalo, called "pounds." In 1876, he signed Treaty Number 6 with the Canadian government, but his band never received the food and farm tools promised in the treaty. The band then gave power to Fine Day, their war chief, who wished to join the Métis's fight against the government. Poundmaker opposed this, but the Canadian government accused him of treason anyway. He turned himself in and was found guilty at his two-day trial in 1885. Although he was sent to prison for three years, he was released early because of illness and died soon after in 1886.

Traditional Way of Life

At first, Cree babies were carried in a hide sack stuffed with moss. The introduction of the cradleboard gave the Crees another way to carry their babies.

Western Woods Cree Traditional Culture

When a Western Woods Cree child came into the world, there was little ceremony. Named several months after birth by an older person, the baby was often kept on a cradleboard with moss diapers. Young children were allowed to do as they liked, but as they grew older, they had to help their parents.

Western Woods Cree teenagers fasted alone for a short time to gain powers from the spirits that appeared in their dreams or **visions**. When a boy killed his first big-game animal, such as an elk or moose, at about age fourteen, a feast was held in his honor. A girl reaching **puberty** stayed in a small lodge away from camp for four nights with a wise old woman to keep her company and tell her stories. She returned to camp to attend a feast in her family lodge.

This early illustration of the Cree people shows life inside a traditional dwelling. The people warm themselves by the fire, which also cooks the meal in a pot and dries the meat hanging on a pole above.

Moving with the Seasons

The land of the Western Woods Crees is cold much of the year, so they traveled on snowshoes and toboggans during the long winter, as well as by canoes and dog **travois** in the summer. When everything froze, activity slowed, except when the men went hunting and trapping occasionally. Then, in spring, the Crees sprang into action for great caribou hunts. As soon as the rivers thawed, Cree bands paddled canoes to their summer camp, gathering at a lakeshore for fishing, berry picking, and visiting. By autumn, the bands would leave by canoe and scatter to their winter hunting grounds.

Daily Life

While the women set up camp, prepared meals, and took care of the young children, the men hunted and trapped caribou, moose, beaver, duck, and other game animals. Cree lodges — made of caribou hides covering a framework of wooden poles — provided shelter. Often decorated with porcupine quills or beads, most Cree clothing was made from the tanned hides of moose, caribou, and elk. Men wore moccasins, leggings, overshirts down to their knees, hats, mittens, and cloaks or blankets of beaver, caribou, or otter skins. Women dressed in moose-hide dresses and all of the same warm outerwear as worn by the men.

Body Decoration

Western Woods Crees used both tattooing and body paint as decoration. The men usually tattooed their chest and arms; women tattooed lines from their lower lip to their chin. Usually lines or shapes, the tattoos were made by putting a charcoal paste on the skin and then pricking it with needles. People painted their face with designs or with realistic figures, often using the color red.

A fire-making utensil case displays the beautiful decorative beadwork done by women on household items and clothing. Decorative work and tattooing often filled the time spent inside the lodges.

When the Western Woods Cree bands gathered together in the summertime, they worked hard but had a lot of fun. They played many games; both foot and horse races were popular. In the evenings, they told stories and sometimes held feasts and dances. Often the Crees painted and tattooed their faces and bodies with beautiful designs.

Government and Religion

The Western Woods Crees were organized into bands made up of family members; they had no formal government. Leaders were men chosen for their hunting ability, experience, and spiritual power. They tried to influence people's behavior but did not control it.

The Crees have kept many of their traditional religious beliefs private. They believed in a Great Spirit and feared the Windigo, a creature with a heart of ice and a taste for human flesh. The Crees believed that sickness and injuries were the results of evil spirits at work. Helping spirits, or manitous, came to them in dreams or visions and gave them special powers or protection for hunting or warfare.

Animals had spirits, too. The Crees believed that during the hunt, the hunter made a connection with the animal being hunted, and the animal decided whether or not to give itself to the hunter.

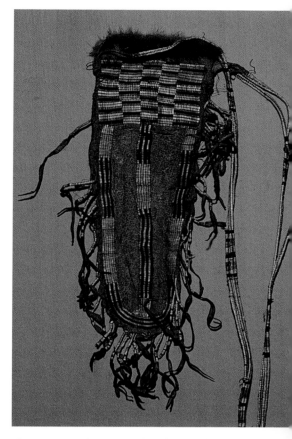

A copper hunting knife (left) and its beaded case are typical of the tools used by the early Crees.

The Winter Windigo

A horrible creature, the gigantic Windigo comes at wintertime. Once a normal human being, the Windigo was taken over by a savage spirit and now wants to eat other humans. Though hairy on the outside, his body has ice on the inside. Only a medicine man or someone with special powers can kill a Windigo; that person must make sure to burn the Windigo as well so its heart of fire can be destroyed by fire.

Plains Cree Traditional Life

Soon after the birth of a Plains Cree baby, a medicine man or woman would name him or her, based on a vision or dream, at a feast. Parents might use a different "everyday" name with their child to protect its sacred given name.

Older children spent most of their time with their grandparents, who told them stories and taught them basic life skills. Teenage boys taught the younger ones how to hunt and fight. When girls went through puberty, they remained alone for four nights for their vision quest. Teenage boys also went on vision quests to seek spirit power, spending several nights alone while fasting. During a dream or vision, an animal spirit helper would appear, describe the gifts being given to the young man (such as the ability to lead war parties,

A modern Cree medicine man, Oo-chin-a-pees. Keepers of traditional ways, Cree medicine men help heal people and provide spiritual leadership.

cure the sick, or hunt buffalo), and teach him a power song.

The most important Plains Cree ceremony was the Sun Dance, given to honor the thunder or the sun. Also called the "Thirsting Dance" by the Crees, the participants did not eat or drink during the four-day ceremony but sang and danced throughout, concentrating

A braid of dried **sweetgrass** is burned, and the smoke purifies the people who breathe it.

A key religious ceremony, the Sun Dance was also a social event for the Cree people that featured dancing, gambling, and courting.

on keeping sacred promises, or vows, that were made to the spirits. During the Smoking Spirit ceremony, another important event, an all-night singing session honored all the spirits. Buffalo dances were held to assure large herds and good hunting. The Crees smoked a pipe as an offering to the **supernatural** and used sweat baths and the smoke from burning sweetgrass to clean and purify themselves.

Shaking Tent

"Shaking tent" or "shaking lodge" is a practice in which a special medicine man enters a tent or lodge alone in order to speak with the spirits and find out the answers to questions that the people sitting outside might have. For example, if the hunters want to know where the buffalo are, the spirits are consulted. When the spirits enter the tent to speak with the medicine man, they cause the tent or lodge to move or sway from side to side.

A Cree chief, Broken Arm (also known as He-Who-Has-Eyes-Behind-Him) visited Washington, D.C., in 1831, where George Catlin painted his picture.

Plains Cree Government

The Plains Crees were organized in groups of small bands, some of which had more than one chief. Councils of leading men made decisions for the band. Basing their decision on the chief's hunting ability, wealth, and generosity, people chose the band they wanted to join. Each band had a warrior society, to which most of the younger men belonged. The warrior society gave food to needy people and organized the large buffalo hunts.

Depending on the Buffalo

Buffalo hides provided both clothing and shelter for the Plains Crees. Men wore hide breech-cloths and leggings; women's dresses were also made of hide and decorated with beads or embroidery. Hide tepees provided housing.

During the winter, the Crees wore mittens and moccasins made from hide and decorated with beadwork.

This shirt, decorated with battle scenes, was worn by a Plains Cree man on special ceremonial occasions.

Most of the food was based on the buffalo; when there was no fresh meat, the Crees ate **pemmican**. A typical Plains Cree meal was soup made from meat, fat, berries, and turnips. When the hunting was poor, the men fished and the women picked berries and dug wild turnips. Collecting maple sap, they made it into syrup and sugar.

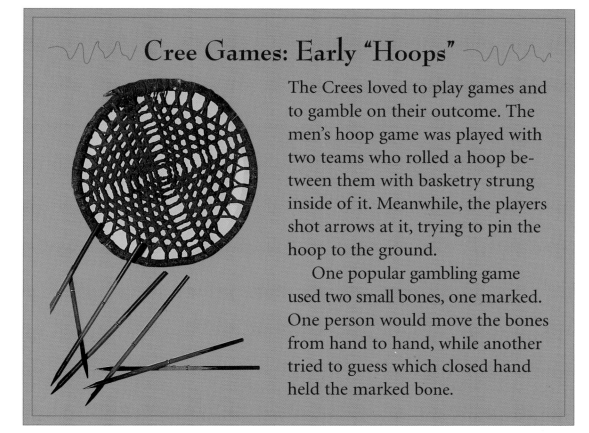

Cree Games: Early "Hoops"

The Crees loved to play games and to gamble on their outcome. The men's hoop game was played with two teams who rolled a hoop between them with basketry strung inside of it. Meanwhile, the players shot arrows at it, trying to pin the hoop to the ground.

One popular gambling game used two small bones, one marked. One person would move the bones from hand to hand, while another tried to guess which closed hand held the marked bone.

Today

> How can we
> be discovered when
> we were already here?
>
> *Jane Ash Poitras,
> Cree artist*

Contemporary Literature and Arts

Cree people participate in all of the modern arts as well as continuing to work in traditional styles. Along with paintings and sculptures, Cree artists create moccasins, complex beadwork, and birch-bark boxes.

Author and artist George Littlechild illustrates children's picture books that he and others have written. One example is *This Land Is My Land,* a book that describes his experience of growing up as a Cree boy in Canada in colorful images and words.

Kent Monkman is a Cree painter and filmmaker who liked to paint and draw as a young boy. Now he uses Cree symbols — invented by a missionary in the late 1800s to express the Cree language — in a series of paintings called *The Prayer Language.* His first film, *A Nation Is Coming,* won several awards. He is working on more paintings and films that express a Native point of view.

Jane Ash Poitras is a famous Cree artist whose paintings hang in U.S. and Canadian museums. Her latest work is a large exhibit that took three years to create. Called *Who Discovered the Americas?,* this mixture of photos and paintings shows the effects of Columbus's "discovery" on Native Americans.

Working Together

During the last half of the twentieth century, European Canadians spread into traditional Cree hunting grounds and

Buffy Sainte-Marie

Born February 20, 1941, on a Cree Reserve in Saskatchewan, Canada, Buffy Sainte-Marie became a world famous folksinger. While attending college, she became a popular singer on campus and in clubs. Sainte-Marie built a huge international following in the mid 1960s and became famous for an antiwar song called "Universal Soldier." During her career, she wrote over two hundred songs and recorded more than fifteen albums. In 1976, she left the music business to work as a teacher and an artist. She still does both and lives in Hawaii.

Buffy Sainte-Marie has lived on many Native American/First Nation reservations during her life.

homelands, disturbing the Crees' traditional way of life. Instead of roaming the forests, Crees settled permanently onto numerous scattered reserves (reservations) in Canada and even one in the United States, as well as in many different Canadian cities and towns. They began to rely upon the Canadian government to provide education, housing, food, and medical care.

Realizing that the Canadian government had not followed through on its treaty promises, Crees became politically active in the 1960s. Plains Cree John Tootoosis founded and led the Federation of Saskatchewan Indians in 1958 and was active in the

Members of the National Indian Brotherhood and the Association of Indians meet together to discuss Cree land issues on November 19, 1974.

National Indian Brotherhood. These and other **activist** groups have worked hard to ensure that the Canadian government fulfilled all of the rights listed in the treaties signed in exchange for Cree land.

Today, an organization called the Cree Nations Confederacy includes all Crees in one group. The Crees now divide themselves into four distinct cultural groups: Plains Crees (who live in central Alberta), Woodland Crees and Swampy Crees (in northern Manitoba), and Moose Crees (Hudson Bay area). The Cree Nations Confederacy works to preserve Cree culture, language, traditions, customs, and traditional lands. They also try to ensure that the Crees are treated as a separate nation.

When you're in the bush, you're not just there to learn how to set a trap, how to hunt moose and caribou or how to set a net. It's about how you take care of yourself and how you deal with yourself in your life.

Robert Jimiken, a senior Cree hunter and trapper, 1998

A Culture's Rebirth

Modern Cree children benefit from band and government programs to encourage Cree culture. Special Head Start Programs teach youngsters traditional singing, drumming, storytelling, and language in preschool. Many elementary schools teach

A Cree bush camp near Hudson Bay contains a mixture of traditional and modern objects. The lodge and stacked firewood contrast with the racy red snowmobile.

kindergarten through third grades only in Cree, and some children now speak the language better than their parents. Other schools have hired Cree elders to advise them and hold powwows, feasts, and round dances during the school year. Cree groups sponsor older children in Cree culture camps during the summer, where they learn the skills needed to live off the land, or "bush skills," just as their great-grandparents had practiced.

In a bush camp near the Great Whale River, Cree women cook in the lodge just as their great-great-grand-mothers did.

A Canadian road sign tells drivers to stop in English, Cree symbols, and French.

During a visit from Great Britain's Prince Charles, Cree women dress in their finest traditional clothes to honor him.

Contemporary Cree Issues

During the 1990s, the Canadian First Nations (including the Crees) and the Canadian government worked together to review the original treaties signed and settle any remaining treaty issues. This has resulted in many Cree bands signing a "Treaty Land Entitlement Agreement" and gaining additional lands in order to fulfill the original treaty agreement. Not all Cree bands have completed this process yet; it will probably take years.

More than one hundred years after Poundmaker was convicted of treason for his part in the 1885 rebellion, a Canadian television show has questioned Poundmaker's conviction. The show, which aired in October 2002, used the original trial **transcripts** to re-create Poundmaker's trial on film. The filmmakers say that the historical records show that Poundmaker was innocent, and they have asked the Canadian justice department to review his case.

The Crees continue to fight to maintain their traditional culture and teach their children the Cree language and the importance of living off the land. The difficulty of balancing a life as a wage earner and the desire to go out into the bush to hunt and trap is an issue most Crees face today, since few can make their living as full-time hunters and trappers. As their prosperity and education increase, the Crees have more choices, and they are choosing to embrace their traditional culture and values whenever they can.

James Bay Hydroelectric Project

In 1971, Quebec's premier, Robert Bourassa, began the James Bay Project hydroelectric dam, which flooded the rivers where the Crees still hunted and trapped. The Crees went to court to protest, and the judge agreed with the Crees. The rest of the project was stopped for twenty years.

In 1991, a different court allowed part of the project to continue, but it looked as if the whole project would never be completed due to the Cree protest. In 2002, however, Cree chief Ted Moses agreed to let Quebec finish the project, which will result in two huge dams to supply Quebec with electricity and provide jobs for the Crees. The project will also pay the James Bay-area Cree bands $44 million a year for fifty years.

This photograph of the James Bay Hydroelectric Project, taken from the air, shows how huge the dam is and how large the area it affects.

However, even more traditional hunting, fishing and trapping grounds will be flooded. In addition, mercury, a poisonous metal, in the ground dissolves into the water and is absorbed by the fish, which have sickened some of the Crees who have eaten them. While the James Bay Hydroelectric Project is a blow to the Cree traditional lifestyle, the Cree bands are hoping that the payments and jobs will give them some new opportunities.

Time Line

1600	Cree population totals fifteen thousand.
1670	Hudson's Bay Company sets up trading posts in Cree territory.
1670–1810	Crees expand their territory and the Plains Cree lifestyle begins.
1781	Smallpox epidemic kills many Crees.
1810–50	Plains Cree Horse Wars.
1870	Canada purchases land from Hudson's Bay Company.
1871	Blackfeet defeat Plain Crees at the Battle of Old Man River.
1876	Poundmaker becomes chief of a Cree band.
1876–1906	The Cree bands sign treaties with the Canadian government.
1884–1921	Sun Dance is outlawed in Canada
1885	Louis Riel leads the Métis against the Canadian government; a Cree sympathizer, Poundmaker is found guilty of treason.
1940s–70	Cree children are sent to boarding schools to learn English.
1958	John Tootoosis and others found Federation of Saskatchewan Indians.
1971	Quebec begins James Bay hydroelectric dam project; Crees protest.
1984	The Chippewa-Cree tribe of the United States creates the Stone Child Community College.
1990s	Canadian First Nations and Canadian government review original treaties and try to settle remaining issues.
2002	Cree agreement with Quebec allows James Bay hydroelectric dam project to be finished.

Glossary

activist: someone who believes in direct action to support or oppose a controversial issue.

convert: to cause a person to change a belief, usually a religious one.

descendants: all of the children and children's children of an individual.

dialects: types of language that are spoken by particular groups or in particular areas.

epidemic: a sudden increase of a rapidly spreading disease.

missions: churches or other buildings where people of one religion try to teach their beliefs to people of another religion.

nation: people who have their own customs, laws, and land separate from other nations or peoples.

pemmican: a food made from dried meat pounded into powder and mixed with melted fat.

puberty: the time of physical changes in the human body when a girl becomes a woman or a boy becomes a man.

reserves or reservations: land set aside by the government for specific Indian tribes to live on.

smallpox: a disease that causes a high fever and small bumps.

social services: services provided by the government or other organizations to help the poor or sick.

supernatural: beyond the natural world; something that cannot be seen, especially relating to gods and spirits.

sweetgrass: a hardy grass that smells like vanilla when dried.

transcripts: exact records, in writing, of an event.

travois: a long sled formed by two poles with a platform between them.

treason: the act of betraying one's country.

treaties: agreements among two or more nations.

visions: things seen or experienced that are not from this world but the supernatural one; they resemble dreams, but the person is awake.

More Resources

Web Sites:

http://www.creeculture.ca Follow the links to learn more about the Cree people, their language, arts, and traditional ways.

http://www.historytelevision.ca/chiefs/htmlen/cree/default.asp Listen to the words of Poundmaker and find out more about other important Crees and Cree culture. Includes maps and time line.

http://collections.ic.gc.ca/games/index.html All about the games of the Plains Crees. Click on different links to learn about Cree ball games, toys, and games of chance and skill.

http://collections.ic.gc.ca/nilhinimuk A visual record of northern Manitoba's Cree People.

Books:

Littlechild, George. *This Land Is My Land*. Children's Book Press, 1993.

Riehecky, Janet. *The Cree Tribe* (Native Peoples). Bridgestone Books, 2003.

Robinson, Deborah B. *The Cree of North America* (First Peoples). Lerner Publications Co., 2001.

Siy, Alexandra. *The Eeyou: People of Eastern James Bay* (Global Villages). Dillon Press, 1993.

Cree Clothing

Read about the different kinds of clothing worn by the Western Woods Crees and the Plains Crees. Draw a picture showing the differences in clothing between the Cree cultural groups. Why did they dress differently? Why do they wear the kinds of clothes that they do?

Honoring a Treaty

In the 1870s, many Cree bands signed treaties with the government, giving up their traditional lands for assigned reservations and social services such as food, tools, schools, and doctors. What can the Crees do if the government doesn't keep its side of the bargain? Form a small discussion group and discuss what you think their choices are.

Role Playing

Poundmaker was accused of treason, or disloyalty to the government, because of his part in Riel's rebellion. In a group, act out the trial with students taking the part of the two lawyers, the judge, and Poundmaker. Other students can be the jury. What do you think each of these people was thinking and feeling during the trial?

Name Yourself

Plains Cree children often had two names: their "real" name and an everyday name that was descriptive of what they looked like, what they were good at, or something that happened to them. If you were a Plains Cree, what do you think your everyday name would be and why? Write a paragraph explaining your name.

Index

arts, 22, 23

beliefs, 4, 8, 13, 14, 17, 18–19
Big Bear, 12
Blackfeet, 10, 11
body decoration, 16
Bourassa, Robert, 27
buffaloes, 10, 11, 13, 19, 20–21

Canadian government, 9, 11, 12,
    13, 23, 26
ceremonies, 13, 18–19
children and teenagers, 14, 15,
    18, 24
clothing, 9, 11, 15, 20
Cree Nations Confederacy, 24

diseases, 7, 8, 17

farming, 11
Federation of Saskatchewan
    Indians, 23
Fine Day, 13
fishing, 6, 27
food, 6, 21

games, 16, 21
government, 16, 20

horses, 11
housing, 11, 15, 20
Hudson's Bay Company, 7
hunting and trapping, 6, 7, 8, 10,
    14, 15, 17, 20, 21, 23, 26–27

James Bay hydroelectric dam, 27

language, 5, 6, 9, 22, 24, 25, 26
literature, 22
Littlechild, George, 22

medicine men, 17, 19,
Métis, 12, 13
missionaries, 8, 12
Monkman, Kent, 22
Moses, Ted, 27

National Indian Brotherhood, 24

origin story, 4

Plains Crees, 5, 10–13, 18–21
Poitras, Jane Ash, 22
Poundmaker, 12, 13, 26

Riel, Louis, 12

Sainte-Marie, Buffy, 23
schools, 8, 9, 11, 13, 24, 25
social services, 8, 13
Sun Dance, 13, 18

Tootoosis, John, 23
trading, 6, 7, 9, 10
treaties, 8, 11

warriors, 12, 20
Western Woods Crees, 5, 6–9, 14–17
Windigo, 17